# HOW TO REALLY LOVE YOUR WIFE

# How to
## *Really Love*
# Your Wife

---

*Love-in-Action Ideas for Every Day*

---

## H. NORMAN WRIGHT

**Servant Publications**
Ann Arbor, Michigan

Vine Books is an imprint of Servant Publications especially designed to serve evangelical Christians.

Published by Servant Publications
P.O. Box 8617
Ann Arbor, Michigan 48107

Scripture quotations in this book have been taken from various translations of the Bible, including Holy Bible, New International Version (NIV), The New King James Version of the Bible (NKJV), and the Living Bible (LB), as noted in the text. All rights reserved.

Cover design by Hile Design and Illustration

96 97 98 99  10 9 8 7 6 5 4

Printed in the United States of America
ISBN 0-89283-886-8

```
Library of Congress Cataloging-in-Publication Data

Wright, H. Norman
How to really love your wife : love-in-action ideas for every day / H.
Norman Wright.
     p.   cm.
ISBN 0-89283-886-8
1. Marriage—Miscellanea.   2. Love—Miscellanea.   3. Wives—
Psychology—Miscelanea.   I. Title.
HQ734.W94917   1995
248.8'425—dc20                                    95-12248
                                                      CIP
```

### 1

Take on the roles of both student and teacher in
your marriage. A fulfilled marriage is one in which
husband and wife teach one another and
learn from one another.

### 2

Don't compete with your wife—be her friend.
Wish her the best and be enthusiastic about
her achievements. Brag about her!

### 3

Pray together often. "It is only when a husband and wife pray together before God that they find the secret of true harmony, that the difference in their tastes enriches their home instead of endangering it."[1]

### 4

It's not your job to "reform" your wife. Encourage her, praise her, resolve to never take her for granted, and leave the work of transformation up to the Holy Spirit.

### 5

Remember: There is no perfect wife,
perfect husband, or perfect marriage.

### 6

Silence is not always golden, especially between
husband and wife. Ask your wife when she'd
like to set aside time just to talk.

### 7

Disagreeing with your wife is one thing; behaving
disagreeably is another. Tell her that you love
her even if you don't see eye to eye.

### 8

Ask your wife what three words she'd like you to
drop from your vocabulary—then do it!

### 9

Flowers are never a substitute for the words
"I love you and I want to hear what
you have to say." Give both!

### 10

Find a recording of your wife's favorite romantic song
and play it for her. Ask her what sounds she finds most
soothing and romantic and provide them for her.

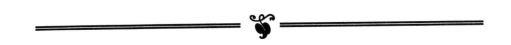

### 11
Realize that sometimes your love for your wife will be
a decision instead of a strong feeling. That's mature,
lasting love. That's *agape* love.

### 12
Fantasizing in marriage is healthy as long as a hus-
band's mind is filled with visions of his wife.
Fantasize about your wife!

### 13
Are you predictable? Do you always follow the
same routine? Make something new happen
in your relationship with your wife today.
Go ahead—surprise her!

### 14

When you love your wife, you take her feelings and
viewpoints seriously even when they differ from
your own. When you disagree, tell her,
"I see things differently, but maybe I
can learn from you." Believe it!

### 15

A baseball team doesn't stop working after winning one game. Winning a woman to be your wife doesn't mean you stop winning her after marriage.

### 16

Lectures belong in the classroom, not in the home. Sacrificial love doesn't demand; it respectfully asks.

### 17

Genuine love for your wife is incompatible with jealousy, envy, or bitterness. Those responses will push her away rather than draw her close to you.

### 18

Recognize that expressing your anger is not necessarily bad; it's *how* you express your anger that makes the difference.

## 19
Does your wife feel nourished and built up during the time you spend at home? Ask her!

## 20
Ask your wife, "What do you want to be doing five years from now? Ten years from now? How can I help you achieve that?"

### 21
Settle issues in your marriage as soon as they come up.
"Harmony in marriage exists when there is an
absence of unsettled issues and offenses
between the two of you."[2]

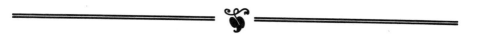

## 22
Blame in a marriage may identify responsibility, but it does nothing to bring about reconciliation.

## 23
Fault-finding deeply wounds a wife. Sincere praise, the words "thank you," and nonsexual touches nurture her.

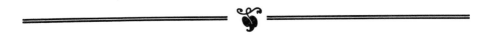

### 24
Tell your wife how much you value her. "A wife of noble character, who can find? She is worth far more than rubies. Her husband has full confidence in her and lacks nothing of value" (Proverbs 31:10-11 NIV).

### 25

Don't stop at complimenting your wife once. Look
for something else nice to tell her. She needs
at least one compliment a day!

### 26

Work at understanding your wife. When she feels
understood, she will feel secure in your love
and respond to you in kind.

### 27
Be willing to do some things the way your wife does them. Put the dishes in the cupboard her way or fold her socks the way she does, just to please her.

### 28
Keep in mind the reasons you work at your job or career. "It is not what a man does that determines whether his work is sacred or secular, it is why he does it."[3]

### 29

Intimacy in marriage is both sexual and emotional, but emotional intimacy is the prelude to sexual intimacy. Your wife needs conversation and attention every day.

## 30

Nurture friendships with men. Medical research tells us that men who have close friends enjoy life more and live longer. List the close friends in your life and tell them how much you appreciate them.

### 31
Being a friend to your wife means sharing with her the conversations you have in your mind.

### 32
For your next anniversary, give your wife a card listing as many reasons why you're glad you married her as years you've been married.

### 33
According to fishing guides in Alaska, why do women catch more fish than men? Because they listen and follow the guide's instructions better. Hmmmmm....

### 34
Give your wife a day-by-day calendar with a personal message of love written on the first and fifteenth of each month.

### 35

In the midst of personal or family crisis, don't waste energy trying to figure out *why*. Trust God, use your energy creatively, and know that solutions will follow.

## 36

What is God's plan for you and your family at this time? "The will of God grows on you. That which is not of God will die—you will lose interest. But the plan of God will never die."[4]

### 37
Temptation is inevitable, but it's not the problem.
What you *do* with temptation *can* be the problem.
Will you play with it, entertain it, or evict it?

### 38
Memorize a Bible verse with your wife every
two weeks. Learn to say with the poet, "I delight
in your decrees; I will not neglect your word"
(Psalm 119:16 NIV).

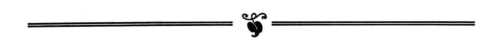

### 39

Talk with your wife about how you see God, who He
is, and what He is like. Ask for her viewpoint.

### 40

Use your competitive spirit to see if you can
"out-serve" your wife. Now there's a goal worth
striving for! Think of three new ways you
can serve your wife this week.

### *41*

Know that you will make mistakes as a husband. Your
wife knows it, and God does, too. Don't give up—
learn from your mistakes and move on.

## 42

Be conscious of your prayer requests. Are your
prayers compatible with the character of God or
would He violate His nature by giving
you what you're asking for?[5]

### 43

Does your wife know you well enough to write your biography from age one to fifteen? If not, help her out. She'll love the time you spend together talking.

### 44

The best way to tell your wife about something you
don't like is to tell her about something you *do* like.
For example: "I really like it when you try
out new recipes on me."

### 45
Treating your wife in loving ways is like putting money
in a savings account. It pays interest.
Make plenty of deposits!

### 46
Before making love with your wife some evening,
read aloud from the Song of Solomon.

### 47

What dreams do you have for your marriage that are
still unrealized? Share them with your wife
and watch them unfold.

### 48

What cripples a marriage is not the problems and
conflicts, but emotional malnutrition brought
on by apathy and indifference.

### 49

The words "If only…" stop action and create worry
and a sense of uneasiness for both you and your wife.
When you feel an "If only" coming on, say instead,
"Let's commit this to the Lord."

## 50

The next time you find yourself arguing with your wife, ask yourself, "Is my goal to punish and dominate my wife, or to understand her?" If needed, redirect your arguments toward the goal of reconciliation.

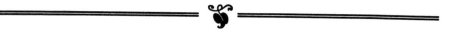

### 51

What gift would your wife never expect from you?
Don't ask her. Figure it out for yourself, then give it.
Watch a new image of you develop in her
heart and mind.

## 52

Differences between you and your wife can either drive you apart and weaken your marriage, or they can help you develop a strength you would never experience any other way. List three ways you and your wife are different and consider how each difference might strengthen your marriage.

### 53

It's been suggested that a woman's basic needs in
marriage are affection, conversation, honesty and
openness, financial support, and family commitment.[6]
Are your wife's basic needs being met?

### 54

When your wife lets you know you've hurt or offended
her, think about your goal and choose your response.
Will you be defensive? Resentful? Humble? Sorrowful?
If your goal is to be close again, the choice is clear.

### 55
For women, emotional loving comes before physical
loving. A wife likes affection even when it has nothing
to do with sex. But nonsexual affection
can lead to great sex!

### 56
Think about spending the extra time you put into
work with your family instead. You may not
accumulate as many things, but investing
in lives pays great dividends.

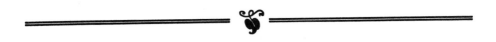

### 57
Purchase a dozen Valentine's cards in February and
send one to your wife each month of the year.

### 58
When your wife is upset, exhausted, or overwhelmed,
do you know what she needs most of all? Usually it's
simple companionship. She doesn't want to feel alone.
Be there for her. Your presence, patience,
and prayers will help her feel loved.

### 59

When you have an important decision to make, first pray for wisdom, then ask your wife for her input. Keep in mind that she may know best!

### 60

Don't look at your marital woes through a telephoto lens, focusing just on the problems. Balance your perspective. List all the positives about your marriage and share them with your wife.

## 61

A wise husband realizes he is incomplete without
his wife, and he lets her know how she supports
and encourages him.

## 62

What does your wife do that makes you feel loved,
valued, and respected? Write it down, wrap the note
around a long stemmed rose, and lay it on her pillow.

### 63

"If you refuse criticism you will end in poverty
and disgrace; if you accept criticism you are on
the road to fame" (Proverbs 13:18 LB). What
accurate criticism has your wife voiced recently
that you haven't accepted? Admit it to
yourself and to her.

## 64
Doing things for and with your wife was part of the
process of falling in love—and it's how you'll stay
in love. Write her a love letter, make her breakfast
in bed, clean the house together.

## 65

Tape-record your conversations with your wife for a week so you can hear what she hears when you talk to her. Is your communication helpful, healing, and sensitive?

### 66

"If you love someone you will be loyal to him no matter what the cost. You will always believe in him, always expect the best of him, and always stand your ground in defending him"
(1 Corinthians 13:7 LB).

### 67

"In buying a gift for your wife, practicality can be
more expensive than extravagance."[7]
Go a little wild!

### 68

You will maintain a close relationship with your wife
only if both of you work to make yourselves
understood. Ask questions, give examples, and
use words and illustrations she can easily relate to.

### 69

Recognize that the responsibility of the marriage is not
yours alone and behave accordingly. Share the
responsibility with your wife, and let her
know you are sharing it.

### 70

Pray, study Scripture, or read devotional materials with
your wife on a regular basis. The closer a man is to
God, the easier it is for him to be open to his wife.

### 71

Recognize that your wife's happiness is tied up in your own. Don't dwell on the negative in your life; create positive experiences to share with her. Be happy!

### 72

Listen to your wife. Sit down, stop what you're doing, and really *listen*. It's the only way to find out what's important to her.

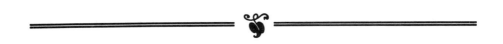

### 73
When your wife asks, "How do I look?" be more
specific than "Fine." How about: "I like the
way you did your hair today," or "The color of
your blouse really makes your eyes sparkle"?

### 74
Give your wife the same attention you give to a
football game or a basketball game on TV. Sometime
ask her what *she* would prefer watching during the
game. This is sacrificial love!

## 75

It's far easier to avoid conflict in marriage than to take
steps necessary to resolve conflict. Avoidance, however,
will only complicate matters. To make conflicts
disappear, face them, discuss them, and look
for creative ways to resolve them.

### 76

To what extent are you irresistible to your wife? To what extent are the two of you still incompatible? Are you moving from incompatibility to irresistibility? Think of three ways to reduce your incompatibility, increase your irresistibility, or both.

### 77

Forgiveness is not a paid-up life insurance policy.
It needs continual investment for a marriage
renewal policy.

### 78

"A word fitly spoken is like apples of gold in settings of
silver" (Proverbs 25:11 NKJV). The translation
for marriage: "The right word at the right
time, how good it is!"

### 79

Allow your wife to be unique. Unless a husband has a
death wish, he knows not to say to his wife, "That's
just like a woman!"

### 80

Sometimes giving your wife a simple hug or holding
her in silence tells her more than words can say.
The right kind of touch says, "I understand.
I accept you the way you are."

*81*

List the experiences in your marriage so far that
you will want to remember twenty-five years
from now. Ask your wife to create a similar
list and share it with you.

## 82

Make the following vow to your wife: "Neither by day nor by night will I ever cut you down in company. Not before my family, your family, our family."[8]

### 83

The quality of your spiritual life will be the remedy for
the aches and pains dispensed by life's stresses. Discuss
your shared spiritual life on a regular basis. Talk about
how you could make it even better.

## 84

If your lines of communication need repair, be your own handyman. You and your wife may need to tear down some walls before you can rebuild the relationship. Set aside ten minutes every day for uninterrupted talk. It's a beginning.

### 85

Sex and verbal communication cannot be separated.
One is not a substitute for the other.

### 86

Keep in mind that love is concern for
what concerns your wife.

## 87

Remember that in a marriage the question is not so much who is right, but what is right for the marriage. Think about it.

## 88

A loving husband helps his wife discover and develop
her potential. Make a list of your wife's strengths.
Ask her to do the same for you and then share
your lists. Let her know you believe in her.

### 89

If you are a fast worker, walker, or talker, recognize
that it's easier for you to slow down than for
your wife to speed up. Stay with her!

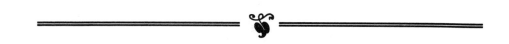

### 90
"In marriage, we must cherish the ability to let loose in reckless displays of affection and admiration."[9]

### 91
Don't suffocate your wife with possessiveness.
Remember that God is the one who owns us;
He has merely entrusted your wife to your care.
Ask her how she would like you to care for her
in new and different ways, then follow through.

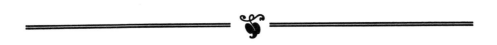

### 92

Invite your wife to a romantic rendezvous by making
a cassette or home videotape. Be creative. Use
background music. She'll love it!

### 93

Complaining about your wife won't improve your
marriage. Instead, tell her what you like about your
marriage and make positive suggestions that
include action on your part as well as hers.

### 94

If your wife doesn't hear you when you say "I love you," it may be that you've been saying it the same way for too long. Say it in a way that will surprise her! Write it on the bathroom mirror or call her on the phone and sing it to her.

## 95

"High blood pressure in marriage is caused by fat clogging the veins of communication."[10]

## 96

One of the greatest gifts you can give your wife is the right to fail and to be imperfect. After all, it's what *you* want from *her*, isn't it?

### 97

If you think you've made some positive changes your wife has requested, evaluate them with *her* measuring stick as well as your own. Ask her what she thinks. Don't argue with her answer.

### 98

"Putting your wife in the Number One slot just below God doesn't shackle you to the house; instead, it frees you of the dread of going home."[11]

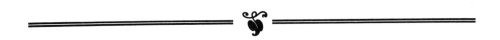

### 99
Volunteer to watch the children for an afternoon or evening and encourage your wife to do something she would enjoy.

### 100
A loving husband is as careful with his wife as he is with his favorite tools, golf clubs, or new car.

### *101*
Have you ever told your wife, "You make me so angry"? Does she really have that much power over you? Is there another possibility? Think about it.

### *102*
Look up I Peter 3:7 to find out every husband's two major responsibilities. Are you doing them?

## 103

Loving your wife means recognizing specific needs and offering to meet them. Be sure to meet her needs in the way she'd like you to. If she needs some time away from the kids, for instance, does she want to leave them at home and go out for the evening, or would she prefer you to take them out so she can get things done at home? If you're unsure, ask.

## 104
Listening to your wife means you're not thinking about your response while she's still talking (Proverbs 18:13). When she finishes talking, summarize what she said to make sure you understood.

### 105

Instead of buying an anniversary card this year, write your own and have it printed on parchment paper.

### 106

What is your plan for ongoing maintenance and renewal of your marriage? This year, read a marriage enhancement book together or attend a marriage class or seminar. Make the arrangements yourself this time.

### *107*

When a husband and wife talk about their thoughts and feelings with each other, every problem is diminished and every joy expanded. Next time, be the one to initiate this kind of sharing.

### *108*

All husbands offend their wives at some point. Some
are oblivious to their wife's hurt, some ignore it,
and some admit their offense and ask forgiveness.
What has been your pattern? Practice asking
forgiveness. It will draw you closer together.

### 109

A meaningful sexual experience for your wife
is related directly to your gentleness with her.
Be gentle in word and touch.

### 110

On a scale of 0 to 10, where would you rate your
marriage today? Where would your wife rate it?
Predict her answer and then (gulp) ask her.

### 111

There are two women in every marriage—a man's wife
and his mother. Your allegiance should be to your
wife. Ask her how you're doing on this one.

### 112

Does the TV in your home build your marriage relationship or detract from it? Ask your wife if she would
agree to keep the television off for a month so you can
both work on your communication with each other.

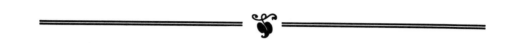

### 113

Change is a vital part of a growing marriage. List three
ways you are different this year compared to last.
Ask your wife what she thinks.

### 114

Talk with your wife about your budget, bank accounts,
and tax returns. Don't "protect" her from your
financial worries; withholding information can
lead to insecurity and mistrust on her part.

### 115

Often when a woman is feeling stressed, she moves toward her husband for comfort. Give your wife a listening ear, a gentle hug, and a strong shoulder—and no advice unless she asks for it!

### 116

Marriage often turns out to be more than you expected. But you and your wife can shape the future of your marriage by determining its direction. List three common goals you and your wife have for your marriage. If you don't have any, don't wait any longer!

### *117*

Forgiveness in marriage is tied to grace rather than
justice. It lets your wife off the hook. It doesn't
make her pay again and again for the same failure.
Forgive and forget.

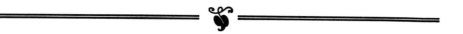

### *118*

When a man loves his wife, he opens himself up to a
new level of hurt. But understand that when a woman
feels unloved by her husband, the pain of her
loneliness is intense. Take the risk. Tell your
wife daily that you love her.

### 119

If you think of your wife as overly talkative, try thinking of her as expressive and thorough instead. Learn
something new from her attention to detail!

### 120

Whenever you think, "I should have listened to her,"
let your wife know. Your standing in her
eyes will increase.

### 121

The marriage relationship is God's way of reflecting his eternal love for his people. What priority should we give to it? What priority do you give to it?

### 122

Listen for God's voice. "And if you leave God's paths and go astray, you will hear a Voice behind you say, 'No, this way; walk here'" (Isaiah 30:21 LB).

### 123
Romance in marriage doesn't just happen; it's something you *make* happen by thought, attention, desire, and action.

### 124
God does not quit on us. A husband's wedding vows to his wife are a reflection of God's pledge to never leave us and never give up on us. What area of your marriage could use more attention and effort?

### 125
Have you ever thought about what your wife might look like twenty years from now, or what you might look like? Talk with her about your thoughts.

### 126
Be careful what you say to your wife in anger. Hurt that comes from angry words can last long after you've forgotten what your anger was all about.

### *127*
Make a list of your needs and ask God to show you
which are important. Let Him decide. Better to lead a
God-centered life than a need-centered life.

### *128*
Think about how much time you spend working.
Tell your wife what your work means to you
and what you would like to be doing in your
work ten years from now.

### 129

Failing doesn't make you a failure in your marriage.
Giving up, withdrawing, viewing yourself as a failure,
and refusing to learn from your experience might!

### 130

A husband doesn't *have* to serve his wife, care for her, help her. He *gets* to! Tell your wife you've learned it's a privilege to love her. Ask how you can serve her even more.

## *131*

In your marital disagreements, do you take the role of
solution-finder or warrior? Only one role allows both
you and your wife to be winners. Warrior isn't it!

### 132

Give your wife the best gift of all: your time and attention. One husband gave his wife a box with a note in it for her birthday. The note read, "I will give you 365 hours this year to talk and share with me. An hour a day. The time is yours."

## 133

Friendship between a husband and wife is rated as the number one reason for marital happiness. Having a close friendship comes from being a good friend. Laughing, playing, talking, and working together builds friendship.

### 134

On a scale of 0 to 10, how important are your possessions to you? "Then [Jesus] said to them, 'Watch out! Be on your guard against all kinds of greed; a man's life does not consist in the abundance of his possessions'" (Luke 12:15 NIV).

### 135

The next time you are sick, notice how you act with
your wife. Are you pleasant or unapproachable?
Are you easy to take care of or should you be
confined to an isolation ward?!

### 136

Never seek guidance from God about something
He has already forbidden in His Word. All we
need to do is be obedient.

### 137

"The only time to stop temptation is at the point of
recognition. If one begins to argue and engage
in a hand to hand combat, temptation
almost always wins the day."[12]

### 138

Men often relate to God in one of four ways: "Give
me," "Use me," "Make me," or "Search me, O God,
and know my heart." Where are you today?

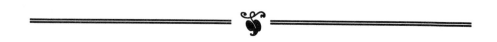

### 139
Ask your wife how you could be better at loving and
serving her. Be ready to hear her answer.
Thank her for her suggestions.

### 140
Don't let the sun go down on your anger.
Resolve your differences as soon as possible—
a great idea in marriage.

*141*
Write your wife a note telling her she's
a memorable person and why.[13]

*142*
Tell your wife on a regular basis, "I love you more
than yesterday and less than tomorrow."

### 143
If your wife ever has an auto accident, *don't* ask
"How's the car?" before you ask, "How are you?!"

### 144
Remind yourself often that husbands who give a little
love find it goes a long way, and husbands who give
a lot of love find it just keeps going and
going and going forever.

### 145

A 50/50 marriage doesn't work; it's too hard to figure out if you and your wife have both come halfway. With a 100/100 commitment, there isn't a question.

### 146

Tell your wife how you see God working in your lives. "Unless the Lord builds the house, its builders labor in vain" (Psalm 127:1 NIV).

### 147

Encourage your wife in specific ways. A woman
who knows her husband supports her will
trust him more and be more open.

### 148

Romance is like a coal that needs your breath and
patience to ignite. If you want a stronger
marriage, take a few breaths and blow!

### 149

Your wife has a love bank. Every time you interact with her you make a deposit or a withdrawal. Have you checked the ledger lately? Keep those books balanced![14]

### 150

When your wife is struggling with a problem, *ask* if she wants suggestions before giving them. If she does, give them gently and lovingly. Be aware of your tone of voice.

### 151

When a husband gives his wife second place—because
he gives his work, sports, or some other interest first
place—she has three choices. She can accept second
place, press for first place and eventually win, or
press for first place until she loses heart.
Why put her through that?[15]

*152*
Ask your wife how the way you handle frustration or
express anger makes her feel and how it affects
your marriage. Ask her how you could
express those feelings differently.

### 153

A great husband is one who can satisfy one woman all his life long—and who can be satisfied by one woman all his life long. It takes effort, time, commitment, and the grace of God, but it's possible. Make this your goal for the life of your marriage.

## 154

If your marriage seems dull, perhaps it's you! Maybe you're stuck in your routine. Maybe you're too predictable. Shock your wife! Be unusually creative and totally unpredictable.

### 155

"Instead of focusing on our mates—how much is lacking—let's look at ourselves and the size of the debt God has forgiven us. Surely he bears with our failings. Let us commit to bear with each other's failings when we are weak and build each other up."[16]

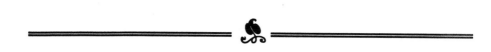

## 156
Talk with your wife on an ongoing basis about how
both you and she would like your marriage to be
different. Listen without defensiveness. Take
time to think about her ideas and yours,
and come back to the discussion later.

### 157

A husband and wife who are friends don't attempt to control or dominate one another. Respect your wife's intelligence and integrity. Ask often, "What do you think?" Say often, "Let's try it your way."

### 158

Begin your day by leaving a note asking your wife how you could be a better listener. Thank her when she responds. Try her suggestions!

## 159

The love-talk that a couple shares before marriage is too often, after marriage, replaced by other kinds of communication. Take time to reflect, then list the things you used to talk about. Ask your wife to do the same. Introduce those topics back into your conversations.

## 160

Talking may not be everything, but it sure beats
avoiding important issues. Avoidance causes
problems to grow. When you find yourself
avoiding your wife, ask yourself, "What is our
disagreement? How can we resolve it?"

### *161*

Conflict can open as many doors as it closes in a
marriage. When you allow it to open a door between
you and your wife, you'll see your differences
disappear. What are some things you can do
to resolve some of your differences? Think
about it and come up with a list of ideas.

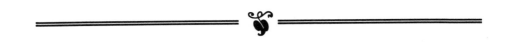

### 162
Love in marriage says, "Will you forgive me for
the hurt I've caused you?" When have you said this?
Do you need to say it now?

### 163
When your wife asks forgiveness for an offense against
you, remember that true forgiveness will elevate her
self-esteem, not depress it. When you tell her you
forgive her, always tell her that you love and
value her as well.

### 164
Before giving your wife advice, ask her if she wants it.
She may just need you to listen.

### 165
When you are silent, does your wife really know what
you're thinking? Or do you just think she does?
Volunteer what you are thinking rather than waiting to
be asked. She'll love you for it.

### *166*

"Sex is a God-ordained means of assuring your partner that she is the most important person in the world right here, right now." Make it creative, romantic, and sensitive to your wife's needs and timing.[17]

### 167
Lines open to God are invariably open to one another,
for a person cannot be genuinely open to God
and closed to his mate.[18]

### 168
When you love and support the best in your wife,
many of the things that irritate you either disappear
or don't bother you as much.

### *169*

Go to the library and check out a book of romantic
poems. Give one to your wife every day in a
hand-written note. Or read one aloud each
day with the lights dimmed.

## 170

When you find yourself arguing with your wife, stop yourself and listen to her. Then respond with, "If I understand your position, you are saying…" and restate what you heard. When you stop to consider both sides of an issue, you'll be amazed how marital discord diminishes.

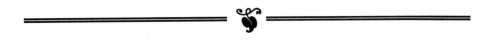

### 171
When your wife has had a bad day, the best words you can say are, "I believe in you, and so does God. What can I do to make the rest of your day easier?"

### 172
Make your wife a priority. It's good for you as well as for her. "The more important a woman feels she is to her husband, the more she encourages him to do the activities she knows he enjoys."[19]

### 173
The purpose for giving your wife a gift is to delight her. Will a season ticket to the football games, a shotgun, or going to a hockey game really delight her? Ask!

### 174
You *can* enjoy shopping with your wife! Plan it in advance as you would a fishing trip.

## 175

When you walk in the door after work, who or what gets your immediate attention? The mail, the cat, the kids, the TV? Your wife wants to be Number One. Before you do anything else, greet her with affection and genuine interest: "I've missed you," "It's good to see you," "Tell me about your day." Avoid "Where's the mail?" or "What's for dinner?" until your wife knows she's the reason you came home!

### 176
Who hears about it when your wife upsets you?
Nobody? Your mother? Your friends? Next time, let
her know directly but calmly that you are upset and
what you would like her to do differently.

### 177
Think of two or three times recently you've shared
with your wife feelings of failure, sadness, or disap-
pointment. If you can't, today's a new day.
Let her see you as you are.

### 178
Make it your business to know at least five of your
wife's needs and how to meet those needs in a way
she desires. Most women, for example, have a
need for affection. It would be difficult
to give too many hugs, cards, or flowers!

### 179
If you're too tired to talk, let your wife know.
Be sure to tell her when you think you'll
be ready to talk to her.

### 180

If your wife tells you she's hurt because you're not talking to her, understand that she may be interpreting your silence as "He doesn't care" or "He doesn't love me." Give her whatever reassurance she needs.

### 181

Satisfied wives have husbands who ask, "Where would *you* like to go on vacation this year?!"
Why not ask her today?

### 182

Scripture teaches us to praise God (Psalm 100:4),
others (Ephesians 4:29), and specifically our wives
(Proverbs 31:28). Think of three ways
you've praised your wife recently.

### 183

Come up with a list of gifts you *think* your wife would
like to receive from you. Show her the list and ask her
opinion. How well did you do? Give her one
of her choices this week.

### 184

Marriage is the best place to alter bad habits or offensive behaviors. Ask your wife if there's anything you do she would prefer you didn't do.

### 185

Be patient before God when the road seems long. "But those who wait on the Lord shall renew their strength; they shall mount up with wings like eagles, they shall run and not be weary. They shall walk and not faint" (Isaiah 40:31 NKJV).

### 186

Love can die when a husband and wife forget how to talk to each other, when they don't make time for romance.[20] Surprise your wife this week with a romantic evening you plan yourself.

### 187

"May your fountain be blessed, and may you rejoice in the wife of your youth" (Proverbs 5:18 NIV). Think of three reasons you rejoice over the woman you married and give her a special card expressing these.

### 188

Lead your wife with love. Don't play the part of a
general commanding the troops or an animal
trainer snapping his whip.

### 189

Being your wife's friend means encouraging her to
reach her potential and delighting in her success as if
you had hit a home run in the World Series. Think of
a personal goal your wife has recently achieved and
plan a celebration with a few close friends.

### 190

Feeling trapped? When everyone in your life is demanding a piece of you and there isn't enough to go around, slip away for a quiet conversation with someone you know will just listen. How about God?

### 191

If your work were taken away from you for the next six months (gulp), how would you feel about yourself? Discuss this question with your wife sometime.

*192*

"A generous man will prosper; he who refreshes others
will himself be refreshed" (Proverbs 11:25 NIV). List
the ways that you are generous toward your wife.
Time? Helping around the house? Money? How else?

*193*

Would you like to discover the will of God for your
marriage? Go before God together. Ask Him what He
wants for your marriage and determine to do it!

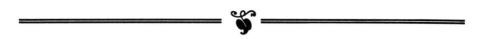

### 194
"If we wait until we have resolved every doubt, every question, before following God, we will never do anything with our life. We must step out by faith."[21]

### 195
Develop an early warning system to combat temptation in your life. Pray together with your wife every day. Memorize 1 Corinthians 10:13 together.

## 196

How does your wife know that you really care for her?
List three specific ways. If you don't know, ask. Then
ask, "How else would you like to be cared for?"

*197*
In one of your braver moments, ask your wife for three
things you could improve on. Tell her you respect
her judgment and you'd like her help in
becoming a better husband.

## 198

Write your wife a note that says, "You just go on getting better every day!"[22] Tape it to the mirror in your bedroom.

## 199

"When our mates have strengths we should affirm them, but never pressure them to perform. To criticize our mates at the point of their strength is to kill their courage."[23]

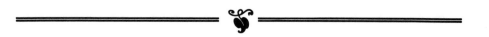

### 200

Many men remember numbers easily: batting averages,
stock market figures, field goal percentages. Do you
know what your wife would like you to remember?
Ask her. Write down specific dates and
occasions and refer to your list!

## 201

An inexpensive gift that gives a thousand percent
return is an activities calendar with "Family Time"
written on several days of each month.

## 202

Remember that love isn't an act; it's a way of life. It's
being there during good times and not-so-good times.
Being there is always possible when Jesus is
invited to be there, too.

### 203

Talk to your wife about her thoughts and concerns
about your marriage. Learn to see life through her eyes
as well as your own. She may see things you miss.

### 204

Some husbands fail to contribute to their wife's
happiness, some actively contribute to her
unhappiness, and some make her feel like
the most important woman on earth.
How does your wife feel?

### 205

Signs that a husband and wife have an intimate relationship: he opens the car door for her; he holds her hand in public; he avoids saying things in front of other people that will embarrass her; he accepts her when she reaches out to him.

How are you doing?

### 206

Take your wife away for a romantic weekend. Tell her
in advance you will not think or talk about work, you
won't discuss problems, and you won't turn on the
TV. Be her servant for the weekend.

### 207
Give your wife a back rub. Brush her hair.
Drop by her office in the afternoon.
Call her just to say, "I love you."

### 208
When your wife wants to talk, turn off or put away
any distractions. Look her in the eye and give her
feedback so she knows you're listening.

### 209

Leave your wife a note in the morning asking her what it is you do that helps her feel close, warm, protected, and understood. Ask her what else you can do.

### 210

Reflect on the ways you communicated with your wife in the early days of your courtship. How did two strangers become intimate friends? Think of three ways you communicate with her now that keeps your intimacy alive. If you can't, ask her for feedback.

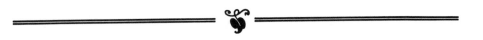

### 211
Listen sensitively. Give frequent feedback. Don't
interrupt, especially to say, "Get to the point!"

### 212
Don't assume you know what your wife is going to say
before she says it. Assumptions lead to distortions, so
listen carefully. She may surprise you!

### 213

Forgive truly. "Forgiving" your wife only if she promises never to fail again is not forgiveness. True forgiveness trusts and believes in the one you love.

### 214

Overlook your wife's shortcomings, but never overlook her potential! Let her know you believe in her. Ask how you can help her reach her goals.[24]

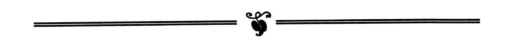

### 215
Tell your wife that she's more important to you than
your work—then find some way to prove it to her!

### 216
Husbands and wives comfort one another in time of
need. How does your wife like you to comfort her?
Don't guess about this—ask if you don't know. How
do you prefer she comfort you? Tell her.

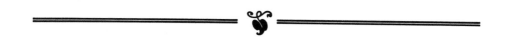

### 217
Remember that your wife's sense of timing is different from your own. If you recover quickly from a quarrel, wonderful—but don't expect her to be there, too. Healing can't be rushed. Give her time.

### 218
Teach your wife gently. Use positive modeling, gentle prodding, encouraging words. Let her know you believe in her.

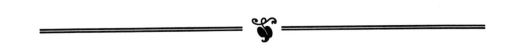

### 219
Be teachable. Listen to your wife, learn from her
positive modeling, accept her gentle prodding.
She believes in you!

### 220
If you haven't already, you will experience the death of
a parent, a close friend, a child, or your spouse. Now is
the time to think about how you will handle it.
Discuss it with your wife.

### 221

Working out a disagreement with your wife?
Attack the problem rather than the person.
Suggest alternatives rather than stubbornly
sticking to your solution as though
it were the only one.

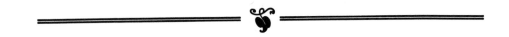

### 222

"Marriage is not so much finding the right person as it is *being* the right person."[25] Are you the husband you wanted to be when you married? If not, it's still possible to become that man.

# NOTES

1. Paul Tournier, *The Healing of Persons* (New York: Harper and Row, 1965), 88-89.
2. Gary Smalley, *If Only He Knew* (Grand Rapids, Mich.: Zondervan, 1979), 75, adapted.
3. A.W. Tozer, *The Pursuit of God* (Harrisburg, Penn.: Christian Publications, 1948), 127.
4. David Wilkerson, *I'm Not Mad at God* (Minneapolis: Bethany, 1967), 32.
5. Richard Exley, *The Making of a Man* (Tulsa: Honor, 1993), 173, adapted.
6. Willard F. Harley, Jr., *His Needs, Her Needs* (Grand Rapids, Mich.: Revell, 1986), 13.
7. Max Lucado, *When God Whispers Your Name* (Dallas: Word, 1994), 43.
8. Charlie Shedd, *Letters to Philip* (Old Tappan, N.J.: Revell, 1968), 64.
9. James R. Bjorge, *Forty Ways to Say I Love You* (Minneapolis: Augsburg, 1978), 24.
10. Bjorge, 59-60.
11. Smalley, 46.
12. Thomas à Kempis.
13. Shedd, 31.
14. Harley, 19, adapted.
15. Patrick M. Morley, *Two Part Harmony* (Nashville: Nelson, 1994), 79, adapted.
16. Morley, 143.

17. Charlie Shedd, *Letters to Karen* (Nashville: Abingdon, 1965), 111.

18. Dwight Small, *After You Say I Do* (Grand Rapids, Mich.: Revell, 1968), 214.

19. Smalley, 47.

20. James Dobson, *Dr. Dobson Answers Your Questions* (Wheaton, Ill.: Tyndale, 1982), 329.

21. Exley, 141.

22. Shedd, *Letters to Philip*, 33.

23. Morley, 143.

24. Bjorge, 30, adapted.

25. Shedd, *Letters to Karen*, 13.